Crime Against Persons with Disabilities, 2009–2013 - Statistical Tables

The rate of violent victimization against persons with disabilities (36 per 1,000) was more than twice the age-adjusted rate for persons without disabilities (14 per 1,000) in 2013. Persons with disabilities experienced 1.3 million violent victimizations, accounting for 21% of all violent victimizations (**figure 1**). Nonfatal violent crimes include rape, sexual assault, robbery, aggravated assault, and simple assault.

The findings in this report are based on the Bureau of Justice Statistics' (BJS) National Crime Victimization Survey (NCVS), a household survey that collects data on U.S. residents age 12 or older (excluding those living in institutions). The NCVS adopted survey questions from the U.S. Census Bureau's American Community Survey (ACS) to identify crime victims with disabilities. The NCVS defines disability as the product of interactions among individuals' bodies; their physical, emotional, and mental health; and the physical and social environment in which they live, work, or play. Disability exists where this interaction results in limitations of activities and restrictions to full participation at school, at work, at home, or in the community. Disabilities are classified according to six limitations: hearing, vision, cognitive, ambulatory, self-care, and independent living.

Data from the ACS were used to estimate age-adjusted victimization rates for persons without disabilities. Unless stated as age-adjusted, findings are unadjusted. For this report, victimization rates were generated by using the ACS population estimates for persons with disabilities. The *Methodology* further details data sources, computational procedures, and data limitations.

The statistical tables in this report detail the level and rates of nonfatal violent victimization against persons with and without disabilities, describe the types of disabilities, and compare victim characteristics. They also include information on the crime incident, such as time of the crime, police notification of the crime, and information on victim services. With the exception of figure 1, all estimates are based on 2-year rolling averages centered on the most recent year. For example, estimates reported for 2013 represent the average estimates for 2012 and 2013. This method improves the reliability and stability of estimate comparisons over time.

FIGURE 1

Annual number of violent victimizations, by victim disability status, 2008–2013

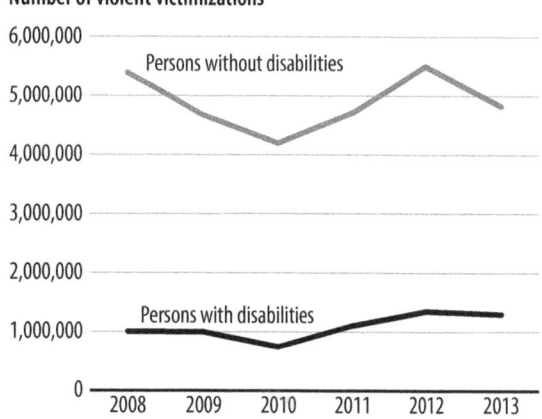

Note: Based on the noninstitutionalized U.S. residential population age 12 or older. See appendix table 1 for estimates and appendix table 2 for standard errors.

Source: Bureau of Justice Statistics, National Crime Victimization Survey, 2008–2013.

List of tables

List of appendix tables

Violent crime by victim's age and disability status

- In 2013, for each age group measured except for persons age 65 or older, the rate of violent victimization against persons with disabilities was at least double the rate for those without disabilities (**table 1**). Among persons age 65 or older, there was no statistically significant difference in the rate of violent victimization by disability status (4 per 1,000).

- Except for persons ages 50 to 64 with disabilities, there was no statistically significant difference in the 2012 and 2013 rates of violent victimization against persons with disabilities for each of the age groups measured. Among persons ages 50 to 64 with disabilities, the rate of violent victimization increased from 2012 (28 per 1,000) to 2013 (42 per 1,000).

The use of age-adjusted rates

The differences in age distributions between the two populations must be taken into account when making direct comparisons of the violent victimization rate between persons with and without disabilities. The age distribution of persons with disabilities differs considerably from that of persons without disabilities, and violent crime victimization rates vary significantly with age. According to the U.S. Census Bureau's American Community Survey (ACS), persons with disabilities are generally older than persons without disabilities. For example, about 42% of persons with disabilities were age 65 or older in 2013, compared to 12% of persons without disabilities (appendix table 18). The age adjustment standardizes the rate of violence to show what the rate would be if persons without disabilities had the same age distribution as persons with disabilities.

TABLE 1
Rates of violent victimization, by victim's disability status and age, 2009–2013

Age of victim	Rate per 1,000 persons with disabilities					Rate per 1,000 persons without disabilities				
	2009	2010	2011	2012	2013	2009	2010	2011	2012	2013
Total	28.9	25.1	26.2	34.2	36.0	23.3	20.2	20.0	22.7	22.9
12–15	106.6	69.9	76.8	122.5	166.1	47.8	34.7	29.9	42.7	52.6
16–19	77.1	101.3	122.9	101.8	75.6	37.2	30.9	37.1	40.7	35.0
20–24	103.8	73.8	105.1	100.6	91.0	39.4	32.8	32.1	36.6	31.9
25–34	49.9	39.5	53.7	82.6	66.6	30.3	29.3	27.7	27.9	30.3
35–49	55.8	48.8	41.5	61.0	59.8	19.9	17.2	18.0	22.1	21.3
50–64	25.5	24.1	20.3	27.9	41.5	11.5	11.3	11.2	11.2	11.9
65 or older	2.8	2.5	4.6	5.9	4.1	4.0	3.8	3.2	4.6	4.5

Note: Based on the noninstitutionalized U.S. residential population age 12 or older. Estimates are based on 2-year rolling averages. See appendix table 3 for standard errors.

Sources: Bureau of Justice Statistics, National Crime Victimization Survey, 2008–2013; and U.S. Census Bureau, American Community Survey, 2008–2013.

Violent crime by type of crime

- The rate of violent victimization against persons with disabilities (36 per 1,000) was more than twice the age-adjusted rate for persons without disabilities (14 per 1,000) in 2013 (**table 2**).

- In 2013, the rate of serious violent victimization for persons with disabilities (14 per 1,000) was more than three times higher than the age-adjusted rate for persons without disabilities (4 per 1,000).

- The rate of simple assault against persons with disabilities (22 per 1,000) was more than twice the age-adjusted rate for persons without disabilities in 2013 (10 per 1,000).

- No statistically significant difference was found in the 2009, 2012, and 2013 rates of violent crime against persons with disabilities. The same pattern was found in the age-adjusted rates of violent crime against persons without disabilities.

- The rate of aggravated assault against persons with disabilities increased from 4 per 1,000 in 2009 to 7 per 1,000 in 2013.

- There was no statistically significant difference found in the 2009 and 2013 rates of rape or sexual assault, robbery, and simple assault against persons with disabilities.

- Serious violence (rape or sexual assault, robbery, or aggravated assault) in 2013 accounted for a greater percentage of violence against persons with disabilities (39%) than violence against persons without disabilities (29%) (not shown).

- In 2013, 24% of violent crime victims with disabilities believed they were targeted due to their disability, an increase from 2009 (13%) (not shown).

TABLE 2
Rates of violent victimization against persons with and without disabilities, by type of crime, 2009–2013

Type of crime	Unadjusted rate per 1,000 persons with disabilities					Age-adjusted rate per 1,000 persons without disabilities*				
	2009	2010	2011	2012	2013	2009	2010	2011	2012	2013
Total	28.9	25.1	26.2	34.2	36.0	13.6	12.2	11.9	13.6	13.7
Serious violent crime	9.0	9.7	11.4	13.1	14.0	4.1	3.8	3.6	3.9	3.9
Rape/sexual assault	1.3	1.0	1.7	2.3	2.0	0.6	0.5	0.4	0.5	0.6
Robbery	3.9	4.1	4.1	5.1	5.3	1.3	1.3	1.3	1.3	1.3
Aggravated assault	3.8	4.7	5.6	5.8	6.6	2.2	2.0	1.9	2.1	1.9
Simple assault	19.9	15.4	14.8	21.1	22.0	9.5	8.4	8.2	9.8	9.9

Note: Based on the noninstitutionalized U.S. residential population age 12 or older. Estimates were based on 2-year rolling averages. See appendix table 4 for standard errors.

*For each year, rates for persons without disabilities were adjusted using direct standardization with the population with disabilities as the standard population. See *Methodology*.

Sources: Bureau of Justice Statistics, National Crime Victimization Survey, 2008–2013; and U.S. Census Bureau, American Community Survey, 2008–2013.

Violent crime rates by sex, race, and Hispanic origin

Sex

- In 2013, for both males and females, the rate of violent victimization was higher for persons with disabilities than the age-adjusted rate for those without disabilities (table 3).

- The unadjusted rate of violent victimization against males with disabilities was 37 per 1,000 in 2013, compared to the age-adjusted rate of 16 per 1,000 for males without disabilities.

- For females with disabilities, the rate of violence was 35 per 1,000 in 2013, compared to 12 per 1,000 females without disabilities.

- In 2013, no statistically significant difference was found in the rate of violent victimization against males with disabilities (37 per 1,000) and females with disabilities (35 per 1,000). However, among persons without disabilities, males (16 per 1,000) had a higher age-adjusted rate than females (12 per 1,000).

- The rate of violence against males with disabilities increased from 26 per 1,000 to 37 per 1,000 from 2009 to 2013. No statistically significant difference was found for females over the same period.

- For males and females with disabilities, there was no statistically significant difference in the 2012 and 2013 rates of violent victimization.

Race and Hispanic origin

- For each racial group measured except for blacks, persons with disabilities had higher age-adjusted violent victimization rates than the age-adjusted rates of persons without disabilities in 2013.

- Among blacks, the apparent difference in the rates of violent victimization by disability status in 2013 was not statistically significant.

- Except for whites, there was no statistically significant difference in the 2009 and 2013 rates of violent victimization among persons with disabilities for each racial group examined.

- The rate of violent victimization against whites with disabilities increased from 28 per 1,000 in 2009 to 38 per 1,000 in 2013.

- In 2013, among persons with disabilities, whites (38 per 1,000) and blacks (31 per 1,000) had higher rates of violent victimization than persons of other races (15 per 1,000).

- There was no difference found in the unadjusted and age-adjusted rates of violent victimization against persons of Hispanic origin with and without disabilities in 2013.

- Among both Hispanics and non-Hispanics, persons with disabilities had a higher unadjusted rate of violent victimization than the age-adjusted rate for persons without disabilities in 2013.

TABLE 3
Rates of violent victimization against persons with and without disabilities, by victim characteristics, 2009–2013

Victim characteristic	Unadjusted rate per 1,000 persons with disabilities					Age-adjusted rate per 1,000 persons without disabilities[a]				
	2009	2010	2011	2012	2013	2009	2010	2011	2012	2013
Total	28.9	25.1	26.2	34.2	36.0	13.6	12.2	11.9	13.6	13.7
Sex										
Male	25.9	22.9	25.8	37.0	37.1	15.8	13.7	14.4	16.5	15.8
Female	31.5	27.1	26.6	31.6	35.0	11.8	10.9	9.7	11.2	11.9
Race[b]										
White	28.0	23.9	24.9	34.2	37.5	13.6	12.0	11.7	13.5	13.5
Black	31.7	28.0	25.1	30.2	31.1	19.2	18.7	17.5	21.3	21.7
Other[c]	25.3	14.4	22.1	27.1	15.0	4.8	4.8	4.3	5.0	5.7
Two or more races	54.8	83.4	91.1	78.4	76.4	20.1	16.7	24.3	21.9	21.3
Hispanic/Latino origin[d]										
Hispanic/Latino	19.8	24.9	25.0	28.9	35.9	13.5	11.8	12.3	15.8	15.2
Non-Hispanic/Non-Latino	29.9	25.1	26.4	34.8	35.9	13.7	12.3	11.9	13.5	13.6

Note: Based on the noninstitutionalized U.S. residential population age 12 or older. Estimates are based on 2-year rolling averages. See appendix table 5 for standard errors.

[a]For each year, rates for persons without disabilities were adjusted using direct standardization with the population with disabilities as the standard population. See *Methodology*.

[b]Includes persons of Hispanic or Latino origin.

[c]Includes persons identified as American Indian or Alaska Native and Asian, Native Hawaiian, or other Pacific Islander.

[d]Includes persons of all races.

Sources: Bureau of Justice Statistics, National Crime Victimization Survey, 2008–2013; and U.S. Census Bureau, American Community Survey, 2008–2013.

Types of disability

- In 2013, persons with cognitive disabilities (67 per 1,000) had the highest rate of violent victimization among all disability types measured (**table 4**). This was similar to previous years.

- In 2013, persons with hearing disabilities (17 per 1,000) had the lowest rate of violent victimization among the disability types examined.

- Persons with hearing (8 per 1,000), vision (12 per 1,000), and self-care (9 per 1,000) disabilities had similar rates of serious violent victimization in 2013 (**table 5**).

- The 2013 rate of simple assault against persons with cognitive disabilities (42 per 1,000) was at least twice that of any other disability type measured (**table 6**).

- Among both males and females, those with cognitive disabilities had the highest rate of violent victimization among the disability types measured in 2013 (**table 7**).

- In 2013, among males, those with ambulatory disabilities (38 per 1,000) had a slightly higher rate of violent victimization than those with self-care disabilities (24 per 1,000). Among females, those with ambulatory and self-care disabilities had similar violent victimization rates (28 per 1,000 each).

TABLE 4
Rates of violent victimization against persons with disabilities, by disability type, 2009–2013

Disability type	2009	2010	2011	2012	2013
Hearing	16.7	10.6	17.1	20.2	16.9
Vision	28.6	24.9	23.2	25.2	29.8
Ambulatory	20.5	19.7	22.6	30.5	32.2
Cognitive	46.0	43.5	50.5	63.3	66.8
Self-care	18.3	17.8	27.3	27.2	26.0
Independent living	24.4	26.4	25.3	28.6	32.4

Note: Based on the noninstitutionalized U.S. residential population age 12 or older. Estimates are based on 2-year rolling averages. Includes persons with multiple disability types. Age-adjusted rates were not generated by disability types due to differences and limitations with the data for these groups. Rates are per 1,000 persons age 12 or older, except for independent living disability, which is per 1,000 persons age 15 or older. See *Methodology*. See appendix table 6 for standard errors.

Sources: Bureau of Justice Statistics, National Crime Victimization Survey, 2008–2013; and U.S. Census Bureau, American Community Survey, 2008–2013.

TABLE 5
Rates of serious violent victimization against persons with disabilities, by disability type, 2009–2013

Disability type	2009	2010	2011	2012	2013
Hearing	7.3	4.5	8.2	10.7	8.4
Vision	8.6	12.0	10.5	7.7	11.9
Ambulatory	6.2	8.2	10.5	14.5	14.7
Cognitive	12.4	17.9	23.5	23.6	25.1
Self-care	3.9	7.9	12.3	11.2	9.3
Independent living	6.1	10.2	11.6	12.1	13.6

Note: Based on the noninstitutionalized U.S. residential population age 12 or older. Estimates are based on 2-year rolling averages. Includes persons with multiple disability types. Age-adjusted rates were not generated by disability types due to differences and limitations with the data for these groups. Rates are per 1,000 persons age 12 or older, except for independent living disability, which is per 1,000 persons age 15 or older. See *Methodology*. See appendix table 7 for standard errors.

Sources: Bureau of Justice Statistics, National Crime Victimization Survey, 2008–2013; and U.S. Census Bureau, American Community Survey, 2008–2013.

TABLE 6
Rates of simple assault against persons with disabilities, by disability type, 2009–2013

Disability type	2009	2010	2011	2012	2013
Hearing	9.4	6.1	8.9	9.4	8.5
Vision	20.0	12.9	12.6	17.5	17.8
Ambulatory	14.2	11.5	12.1	16.0	17.6
Cognitive	33.5	25.6	27.0	39.7	41.6
Self-care	14.4	9.9	15.0	15.9	16.7
Independent living	18.2	16.3	13.7	16.5	18.8

Note: Based on the noninstitutionalized U.S. residential population age 12 or older. Estimates are based on 2-year rolling averages. Includes persons with multiple disability types. Age-adjusted rates were not generated by disability types due to differences and limitations with the data for these groups. Rates are per 1,000 persons age 12 or older, except for independent living disability, which is per 1,000 persons age 15 or older. See *Methodology*. See appendix table 8 for standard errors.

Sources: Bureau of Justice Statistics, National Crime Victimization Survey, 2008–2013; and U.S. Census Bureau, American Community Survey, 2008–2013.

TABLE 7
Rates of volent victimization, by victim's sex and disability type, 2009–2013

Disability type	Rate per 1,000 males					Rate per 1,000 females				
	2009	2010	2011	2012	2013	2009	2010	2011	2012	2013
Hearing	8.9	10.4	19.4	22.3	14.6	27.1	10.7	14.1	17.2	20.2
Vision	32.2	27.7	21.3	23.6	22.7	25.8	22.6	24.7	26.5	35.5
Ambulatory	18.5	19.3	24.6	39.1	38.2	21.8	19.9	21.2	24.5	28.1
Cognitive	44.0	38.0	49.4	65.6	64.6	47.7	48.6	51.5	61.2	68.9
Self-care	19.1	15.1	33.2	34.6	23.6	17.8	19.6	23.1	21.7	27.8
Independent living	25.6	23.4	21.6	29.3	29.1	23.6	28.4	27.7	28.1	34.6

Note: Based on the noninstitutionalized U.S. residential population. Estimates are based on 2-year rolling averages. Includes persons with multiple disability types. Age-adjusted rates were not generated by disability types due to data differences and limitations for males and females. Rates are per 1,000 persons age 12 and older, except for independent living disability, which is per 1,000 persons age 15 or older. See *Methodology*. See appendix table 9 for standard errors.

Sources: Bureau of Justice Statistics, National Crime Victimization Survey, 2008–2013; and U.S. Census Bureau, American Community Survey, 2008–2013.

Violent crime by number of disability types

- About 51% of violence against persons with disabilities involved victims with multiple disability types in 2013, similar to the percentage found in 2012 (52%), and up slightly from 2009 (41%) **(table 8)**.

- The percentage of serious violence against persons with disabilities involving persons with multiple disabilities has increased slightly from 37% in 2009 to 51% in 2013.

- In 2013, there was no statistically significant difference in the rates of violent victimization in persons with a single disability type (35 per 1,000) and persons with multiple disability types (37 per 1,000) **(table 9)**.

- Persons with a single disability type had a slightly lower rate of rape and sexual assault (1 per 1,000) than those with multiple disability types (3 per 1,000) in 2013.

- The 2013 rate of robbery victimization was slightly higher in persons with a single disability type (7 per 1,000) than in persons with multiple disability types (4 per 1,000).

- The 2013 rates of aggravated and simple assault did not differ by the number of disability types.

- After slightly declining in 2010 and 2011, the rate of violence against persons with a single disability type increased to a similar level found in 2009 (33 per 1,000 in 2009 compared to 35 per 1,000 in 2013).

- The rate of violent victimization against persons with multiple disability types increased from 2009 (24 per 1,000) to 2012 (37 per 1,000) and remained steady through 2013.

TABLE 8
Percent of violence against persons with disabilities that involved victims with multiple disability types, by type of crime, 2009–2013

Type of crime	2009	2010	2011	2012	2013
Total	41.4%	50.7%	56.9%	52.1%	50.5%
Serious violent crime	37.3%	52.4%	60.7%	55.6%	50.7%
Rape/sexual assault	32.1 !	47.8	72.5	79.8	68.1
Robbery	27.3	49.4	61.3	51.0	37.0
Aggravated assault	49.3	56.0	56.9	50.1	56.6
Simple assault	43.3%	49.7%	54.0%	49.9%	50.3%

Note: Based on the noninstituionalized U.S. residential population age 12 or older. Estimates are based on 2-year rolling averages. Persons age 15 or older with multiple disability types have two or more of the following disability types: hearing, vision, ambulatory, cognitive, self-care, and independent living. Persons ages 12 to 14 with multiple disability types have two or more of the following disability types: hearing, vision, ambulatory, cognitive, and self-care. See *Methodology*. See appendix table 10 for standard errors.

! Interpret with caution. Estimate based on 10 or fewer sample cases, or coefficient of variation is greater than 50%.

Source: Bureau of Justice Statistics, National Crime Victimization Survey, 2008–2013.

TABLE 9
Rates of violent victimization, by number of disability types and type of crime, 2009–2013

Type of crime	Rate per 1,000 persons with a single disability type					Rate per 1,000 persons with multiple disability types				
	2009	2010	2011	2012	2013	2009	2010	2011	2012	2013
Total	33.3	24.4	22.4	32.5	35.1	24.3	25.9	30.1	35.8	36.9
Serious violent crime	11.1	9.1	8.9	11.6	13.5	6.8	10.4	14.0	14.7	14.4
Rape/sexual assault	1.7	1.0	0.9 !	0.9 !	1.2 !	0.8 !	0.9	2.4	3.6	2.7
Robbery	5.6	4.1	3.1	4.9	6.6	2.2	4.1	5.0	5.2	4.0
Aggravated assault	3.8	4.1	4.8	5.7	5.7	3.8	5.4	6.5	5.8	7.6
Simple assault	22.2	15.2	13.5	21.0	21.6	17.5	15.5	16.1	21.2	22.5

Note: Based on the noninstitutionalized U.S. residential population age 12 or older. Estimates were based on 2-year rolling averages. Persons age 15 or older with multiple disability types had two or more of the following disability types: hearing, vision, ambulatory, cognitive, self-care, and independent living. Persons ages 12 to 14 with multiple disability types had two or more of the following disability types: hearing, vision, ambulatory, cognitive, and self-care. See *Methodology*. See appendix table 11 for standard errors.

! Interpret with caution. Estimate is based on 10 or fewer sample cases, or coefficient of variation is greater than 50%.

Sources: Bureau of Justice Statistics, National Crime Victimization Survey, 2008–2013; and U.S. Census Bureau, American Community Survey, 2008–2013.

Victim–offender relationship

- A lower percentage of violence against persons with disabilities was committed by strangers (31%) than against persons without disabilities (39%) in 2013 (**table 10**).

- The percentage of violence against persons with disabilities committed by intimate partners declined from 2009 (22%) to 2011 (14%) and remained steady through 2013 (15%).

- In 2013, 41% of violence against persons with disabilities was committed by persons they knew well or by casual acquaintances, compared to 35% of violence against persons without disabilities.

Time of crime

- For violent crime victims with and without disabilities, a higher percentage of the violence occurred during daytime (6 a.m.–6 p.m.) than during nighttime (6 p.m.–6 a.m.) (**table 11**).

- The percentage of violence against persons with disabilities that occurred during the daytime did not significantly change during the study period.

- In 2013, 58% of violent crime against persons with disabilities occurred during the daytime, compared to 53% of violence against persons without disabilities.

TABLE 10
Victim–offender relationship, by victim's disability status, 2009–2013

Victim–offender relationship	Persons with disabilities					Persons without disabilities				
	2009	2010	2011	2012	2013	2009	2010	2011	2012	2013
Total	100%	100%	100%	100%	100%	100%	100%	100%	100%	100%
Intimate partner	22.3	22.0	14.2	15.9	15.3	16.9	16.1	15.3	12.5	11.2
Other relatives	10.5	6.6	11.5	11.5	9.0	5.9	6.6	7.3	6.6	5.6
Well known/casual acquaintances	33.7	38.6	37.9	35.5	41.0	28.5	30.0	29.8	31.1	35.1
Strangers	25.1	24.6	27.2	30.3	30.6	38.0	40.1	38.8	40.3	38.8
Don't know	8.5	8.1	9.2	6.8	4.1	10.8	7.2	8.8	9.5	9.3

Note: Based on the noninstitutionalized U.S. residential population age 12 or older. Estimates are based on 2-year rolling averages. See appendix table 12 for standard errors.

Source: Bureau of Justice Statistics, National Crime Victimization Survey, 2008–2013.

TABLE 11
Time violent crime occurred, by victim's disability status, 2009–2013

Time of crime	Persons with disabilities					Persons without disabilities				
	2009	2010	2011	2012	2013	2009	2010	2011	2012	2013
Total	100%	100%	100%	100%	100%	100%	100%	100%	100%	100%
Daytime (6 a.m.–6 p.m.)	53.7	57.3	60.7	59.3	57.9	54.1	53.0	53.1	54.2	53.2
Nighttime (6 p.m.–6 a.m.)	38.2	38.9	36.2	34.3	35.0	41.6	42.5	42.9	41.9	43.6
Don't know	8.1	3.9 !	3.1	6.4	7.1	4.3	4.5	4.0	3.9	3.2

Note: Based on the noninstitutionalized U.S. residential population age 12 or older. Estimates are based on 2-year rolling averages. See appendix table 13 for standard errors.

! Interpet with caution. Estimate is based on 10 or fewer sample cases, or coefficient of variation is greater than 50%.

Source: Bureau of Justice Statistics, National Crime Victimization Survey, 2008–2013.

Police reporting

- In 2013, 48% of violence against persons with disabilities was reported to police, compared to 44% for persons without disabilities (**table 12**).

- During the study period, the percentage of violent crime against persons with disabilities that was reported to police did not change significantly.

- In 2013, there was no statistically significant difference by victim disability status in the percentage of violence reported to police.

- In 2013, there was no statistically significant difference between the percentages of violence against persons with single disability types (46%) and persons with multiple disability types (49%) being reported to police.

- The percentage of violence against persons with multiple disability types that was reported to the police dropped from 61% in 2009 to 44% in 2012 and remained steady in 2013 (49%).

- In every year studied, the majority of violent crime against persons with disabilities that was reported to police was done so by the victim (**table 13**). This was similar to violent crime victims without disabilities.

- The percentage of violent crime against persons with disabilities that was reported by the victim declined from 71% in 2009 to 58% in 2013.

- While the percentage of violence against persons with disabilities that was reported by other household members and someone official did not change from 2009 to 2013, the percentage of violence reported by someone else increased from 11% in 2009 to 23% in 2013.

TABLE 12
Percent of violent crime reported to police, by victim's disability status, 2009–2013

Victim's disability status	2009	2010	2011	2012	2013
Persons with disabilities	54.3%	47.0%	47.2%	48.6%	47.5%
Single disability type	49.8	47.5	54.8	53.3	45.9
Multiple disability types	60.7	46.5	41.4	44.2	49.1
Persons without disabilities	43.5%	47.5%	50.5%	45.9%	44.2%

Note: Based on the noninstitutionalized U.S. residential population age 12 or older. Estimates are based on 2-year rolling averages. See appendix table 14 for standard errors.

Source: Bureau of Justice Statistics, National Crime Victimization Survey, 2008–2013.

TABLE 13
Person who notified police of violent crime, by victim's disability status, 2009–2013

Person who contacted police	Persons with disabilities					Persons without disabilities				
	2009	2010	2011	2012	2013	2009	2010	2011	2012	2013
Total	100%	100%	100%	100%	100%	100%	100%	100%	100%	100%
Respondent	71.3	79.5	72.3	64.2	57.8	60.8	62.9	61.2	57.8	58.4
Other household member	7.2!	3.0!	3.6	3.7	5.7	10.4	9.4	12.3	13.1	9.6
Someone official	8.0	3.4!	2.4!	3.0	7.1	8.1	9.5	8.4	6.7	8.6
Someone else	10.7	8.3	15.8	21.9	22.5	12.4	10.0	9.5	12.0	13.2
Police were at the scene	2.0!	3.9!	2.6!	4.3!	4.0!	5.8	5.7	4.5	6.7	7.9
Offender was a police officer	--!	--!	--!	--!	0.4!	0.9!	1.2!	1.0!	0.2!	0.3!
Some other way	0.7!	1.9!	3.4!	2.9!	2.6!	1.4	1.2	2.4	2.9	2.0
Don't know	--!	--!	--!	--!	--!	0.1!	0.1!	0.7!	0.6!	--!

Note: Based on the noninstitutionalized U.S. residential population age 12 or older. Estimates are based on 2-year rolling averages. Someone official includes a guard, apartment manager, school official, and other officials. See appendix table 15 for standard errors.

! Interpret with caution. Estimate is based on 10 or fewer sample cases, or coefficient of variation is greater than 50%.

--Less than 0.05%.

Source: Bureau of Justice Statistics, National Crime Victimization Survey, 2008–2013.

- In 2013, the most common reason why violent crimes against persons with disabilities were not reported to police was because they were dealt with in another way (44%) (table 14).

- In 2013, for each reason for not reporting crime to police that was measured, the percentages were similar by victim disability status.

- The percentage of violent crime victims with disabilities whose crimes were not reported to police because they were not important enough to the victim increased slightly from 13% in 2009 to 21% in 2013.

Victim services

- In 2013, violent crime victims with disabilities (12%) were somewhat more likely than those without disabilities (8%) to receive assistance from victim services agencies (table 15).

- Except for 2010, the percentage of violent crime against persons with disabilities in which the victim received assistance from victim services agencies was slightly higher than for those without disabilities in each year studied.

- During the study period, the percentage of violent crime victims with disabilities who received assistance from victim services agencies did not change significantly (between 11% and 15%).

TABLE 14
Reasons for not reporting violent crime to police, by victim's disability status, 2009–2013

Reason for not reporting crime to police	Persons with disabilities					Persons without disabilities				
	2009	2010	2011	2012	2013	2009	2010	2011	2012	2013
Dealt with another way[a]	46.0%	34.5%	39.2%	40.4%	43.6%	38.9%	36.2%	38.2%	40.8%	40.8%
Not important enough to respondent[b]	13.2	12.7	15.2	14.0	21.1	23.5	21.6	21.0	23.1	23.5
Insurance wouldn't cover	--!	--!	--!	--!	0.2!	0.1!	0.3!	0.4!	0.3!	0.1!
Police couldn't do anything[c]	1.3!	1.9!	2.6!	2.8!	1.8!	3.4	4.2	4.5	3.3	3.1
Police wouldn't help[d]	26.3	36.9	23.2	19.1	19.5	21.8	21.8	17.3	21.3	20.2
Other reason[e]	31.2	35.0	37.4	42.4	38.4	28.8	36.0	35.9	30.2	35.0

Note: Based on the noninstitutionalized U.S. residential population age 12 or older. Estimates are based on 2-year rolling averages. Detail may sum to more than total because more than one response was allowed. See appendix table 16 for standard errors.

[a]Includes reported to another official and private or personal matter.

[b]Includes minor or unsuccessful crime, child offender, and not clear if a crime occurred.

[c]Includes did not find out until too late, could not recover or identify property, and could not find or identify offender.

[d]Includes police would not think it was important enough, police would be inefficient, police would be biased, and offender was a police officer.

[e]Includes did not want to get offender in trouble with the law, was advised not to report to police, afraid of reprisal, too inconvenient, did not know why it was not reported, and other reasons.

--Less than 0.05%.

! Interpret with caution. Estimate is based on 10 or fewer sample cases, or coefficient of variation is greater than 50%.

Source: Bureau of Justice Statistics, National Crime Victimization Survey, 2008–2013.

TABLE 15
Percent of violent crime victims who received services from nonpolice victim services agencies, by victim's disability status, 2009–2013

Victim's disability status	2009	2010	2011	2012	2013
Persons with disabilities	15.3%	11.2%	12.3%	13.3%	12.2%
Persons without disabilities	7.3	7.9	7.8	7.2	8.0

Note: Based on the noninstitutionalized U.S. residential population age 12 or older. Estimates are based on 2-year rolling averages. See appendix table 17 for standard errors.

Source: Bureau of Justice Statistics, National Crime Victimization Survey, 2008–2013.

Methodology

Survey coverage

The National Crime Victimization Survey (NCVS) is an ongoing data collection conducted by the U.S. Census Bureau for the Bureau of Justice Statistics (BJS). The NCVS is a self-report survey in which interviewed persons are asked about the number and characteristics of victimizations they experienced during the prior 6 months. The NCVS collects information on nonfatal personal crimes (rape or sexual assault, robbery, aggravated and simple assault, and personal larceny) and household property crimes (burglary, motor vehicle theft, and other theft) both reported and not reported to police. In addition to providing annual level and change estimates on criminal victimization, the NCVS is the primary source of information on the nature of criminal victimization incidents.

Survey respondents provide information about themselves (e.g., age, sex, race and Hispanic origin, marital status, education level, and income) and whether they experienced a victimization. The NCVS collects information for each victimization incident about the offender (e.g., age, race and Hispanic origin, sex, and victim–offender relationship), characteristics of the crime (including time and place of occurrence, use of weapons, nature of injury, and economic consequences), whether the crime was reported to police, reasons the crime was or was not reported, and victims' experiences with the criminal justice system.

The NCVS is administered to persons age 12 or older from a nationally representative sample of households in the United States. The NCVS defines a household as a group of members who all reside at a sampled address. Persons are considered household members when the sampled address is their usual place of residence at the time of the interview and when they have no usual place of residence elsewhere. Once selected, households remain in the sample for 3 years, and eligible persons in these households are interviewed every 6 months either in person or over the phone, for a total of seven interviews.

All first interviews are conducted in person with subsequent interviews conducted either in person or by phone. New households rotate into the sample on an ongoing basis to replace outgoing households that have been in the sample for the 3-year period. The sample includes persons living in group quarters (such as dormitories, rooming houses, and religious group dwellings) and excludes persons living in military barracks and institutional settings (such as correctional or hospital facilities) and persons who are homeless.

In 2007, the NCVS adopted questions from the U.S. Census Bureau's American Community Survey (ACS) to measure the rate of victimization against people with disabilities. The NCVS does not identify persons in the general population with disabilities. The ACS Subcommittee on Disability Questions developed the disability questions based on questions used in the 2000 Decennial Census and earlier versions of the ACS. The questions identify persons who may require assistance to maintain their independence, be at risk for discrimination, or lack opportunities available to the general population because of limitations related to a prolonged (i.e., 6 months or longer) sensory, physical, mental, or emotional condition. More information about the ACS and the disability questions is available on the U.S. Census Bureau website at http://www.census.gov/acs/www/.

Changes to the disability questions in the NCVS and ACS in 2008

In 2008, the U.S. Census Bureau changed some of the disability questions on the ACS. The question about sensory disability was separated into two questions about blindness and deafness, and the questions about physical disability asked only about serious difficulty walking or climbing stairs. Also, questions on employment disability and going outside of the home were eliminated in 2008. Census Bureau analysis of 2007 and 2008 ACS disability data revealed significant conceptual and measurement differences between the 2007 and 2008 disability questions. The Census Bureau concluded that data users should not compare the 2007 estimates of the population with disabilities and those of later years. Because the 2007 and 2008 NCVS disability questions mirrored the ACS, estimates of victimization of people with disabilities from the 2007 and 2008 NCVS should not be compared. As a result, the 2007 disability data are not presented in this report. Further explanation about incomparability of the 2007 and 2008 ACS disability data is available at http://www.census.gov/acs/www/Downloads/methodology/content_test/P4_Disability.pdf.

Definitions of disability types

Disabilities are classified according to six limitations: hearing, vision, cognitive, ambulatory, self-care, and independent living.

- *Hearing limitation* entails deafness or serious difficulty hearing.

- *Vision limitation* is blindness or serious difficulty seeing, even when wearing glasses.

- *Cognitive limitation* includes serious difficulty in concentrating, remembering, or making decisions because of a physical, mental, or emotional condition.

- *Ambulatory limitation* is difficulty walking or climbing stairs.

- *Self-care limitation* is a condition that causes difficulty dressing or bathing.

- *Independent living limitation* is a physical, mental, or emotional condition that impedes doing errands alone, such as visiting a doctor or shopping.

Disability questions included in the NCVS from 2008 through 2013

Questions 169a through 173

169a. Are you deaf or do you have serious difficulty hearing?

169b. Are you blind or do you have serious difficulty seeing even when wearing glasses?

170a. Because of a physical, mental, or emotional condition, do you have serious difficulty—

- concentrating, remembering, or making decisions?

- walking or climbing stairs?

- dressing or bathing?

170b. Because of a physical, mental, or emotional condition, do you have difficulty doing errands alone, such as visiting a doctor's office or shopping?

171. Is "Yes" marked in any of 169a–170b? (That is, has the respondent indicated that he/she has a health condition or disability?)

172. During the incident you just told me about, do you have reason to suspect you were victimized because of your health condition(s), impairment(s), or disability(ies)?

173. What health conditions, impairments, or disabilities do you believe caused you to be targeted for this incident?

In the ACS, persons ages 12 to 14 are not asked about having an independent living disability and are therefore not included in the populations with independent living disabilities. Even though crime victims ages 12 to 14 receive this question in the NCVS (question 170b), victims ages 12 to 14 who respond affirmatively are excluded from rates of violent victimization against persons with an independent living disability in order to match the age limitations for having an independent living disability in the ACS (age 15 or older). In this report, rates of violence against persons with an independent living disability are per 1,000 persons age 15 or older, compared to rates per 1,000 persons age 12 or older for other disability types. Also, violent crime victims ages 12 to 14 who report in the NCVS that they have an independent living disability and no other disability are classified as not having a disability to be compatible with age limits on disability definitions in the ACS.

Limitations of the estimates

The NCVS was designed to measure the incidence of criminal victimization against the U.S. civilian household population, excluding persons who live in institutions and the homeless. In this report, institutions refer to adult correctional facilities, juvenile facilities, nursing or skilled nursing facilities, inpatient hospice facilities, residential schools for people with disabilities, and hospitals with patients who have no usual home elsewhere. The measures of crime against persons with disabilities (as measured by the NCVS) cover only people with disabilities who are living among the general population in household settings. Subsequently, there is some coverage error in using just the noninstitutionalized population. For example, according to the ACS, about 96% of the 1.3 million people age 65 or older living in institutions had disabilities in 2013 (not shown). Because persons in these facilities would not be covered in the NCVS, estimates of violence against these persons are not counted. The lack of information from the institutions will result in an undercount of violence against persons with disabilities.

Certain aspects of the NCVS design can also contribute to an underestimation of the level or type of violence against persons with disabilities. For example, the survey instruments, modes of interview, and interviewing protocols used in the NCVS may not be suited for interviewing people who have difficulty communicating, especially by telephone. Some people have disabilities that limit their verbal communication and use technology to enhance their ability to communicate, but many people do not have access to such technology.

Proxy interviews may also lead to an underestimate of violence against persons with disabilities. The survey requires direct interviews with eligible respondents and allows the use of proxy interviews with a caregiver or other eligible party in a limited set of circumstances. A proxy interview is allowed when a respondent is physically or mentally incapable of responding. The survey restrictions on proxy interviews were instituted because someone else may not know about the victimization experiences of the respondent, and because the person providing the information via proxy may be the perpetrator of the abuse or violence experienced by the respondent. Because proxy respondents may be more likely to omit crime incidents or may not know some details about reported incidents, the number or types of crimes against persons with disabilities may be underestimated. In 2013, information about 2% of violent crime incidents against persons with disabilities was obtained from proxy interviews. In addition, 80% of the reports of violent incidents against persons with disabilities obtained through proxy interviews were for simple assault, compared to about 62% of reports of violent incidents against persons with disabilities obtained through nonproxy interviews (not shown).

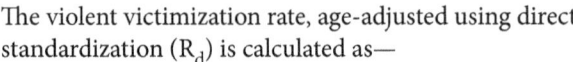

Disability population in the United States

According to the ACS, about 14% of the U.S. population age 12 or older living outside of institutions in 2013 had a disability. Characteristics of the population with and without disabilities are compared in appendix table 18. In 2013, among noninstitutionalized persons with disabilities, 48% were male and 52% were female. Whites accounted for about 77% of the population with disabilities, blacks accounted for 14%, and persons of two or more races accounted for 2%. About 11% were Hispanic. About 42% of the population with disabilities was age 65 or older, compared to about 12% of the population without disabilities. The 2013 ACS population estimates of persons by disability status were generated from Public Use Microdata Sample (PUMS) data.

Public Use Microdata Sample data

To generate populations by disability status for 2008 through 2010, the U.S. Census Bureau generated these estimates for the BJS from the full, confidential ACS dataset. Due to budgetary restrictions, PUMS data from the Census Bureau's ACS were used to calculate populations by disability status for 2011 through 2013. The ACS PUMS dataset is a sample of population and housing unit records from the ACS. Usually, the PUMS files include only about two-thirds of the cases contained in the larger confidential dataset. The ACS PUMS files include the actual responses collected in ACS questionnaires, although some responses have been edited to protect the confidentiality of respondents. The ACS PUMS file included sample weights for each person and housing unit, which were applied to the individual records to expand the sample to estimate totals and percentages of the full population. For more information on PUMS data from the Census Bureau, see http://www.census.gov/acs/www/data_documentation/public_use_microdata_sample/.

Direct standardization

The method used to generate age-adjusted rates of violent victimization of persons without disabilities presented in this report was direct standardization with the population with disabilities as the standard population.[1] Age-adjusted standardization eliminates the problem of different age distributions between and within groups. In general, persons with disabilities are an older population than persons without disabilities. Because crime rates vary by age, direct standardization produces age-adjusted rates for persons without disabilities that would occur if the population without disabilities had the same age distribution as the population with disabilities.

---

[1]For more information on direct standardization, see Curtin, L.R. & Klein, R.J. (1995). Direct standardization (age-adjusted death rates). *Healthy People 2000: Statistical Notes, 6 Revised.* Available at http://www.cdc.gov/nchs/data/statnt/statnt06rv.pdf.

The violent victimization rate, age-adjusted using direct standardization (R_d) is calculated as—

$$R_d = \Sigma\ (w_a * r_a)$$

where

R_d = age-adjusted rate of violent victimization of the population without disabilities calculated using direct standardization

w_a = weight calculated from the population with disabilities for age-group a

r_a = unadjusted rate of violent victimization of persons without disabilities in age-group a

d = direct standardization.

The weight (w_a) for age-group a is calculated as—

$$w_a = n_a\ /\ N$$

where

w_a = weight calculated from the population with disabilities for age-group a

n_a = number of persons in age-group a in the population with disabilities

N = total number of persons in the population with disabilities.

This method produces rates of violent victimization as if the population of interest had the same age distribution as the population with disabilities. To use this method to calculate the violent victimization rate of persons without disabilities, r_a would represent the unadjusted violent victimization rate against persons without disabilities in age-group a.

Change in direct standardization calculations

In previous BJS reports about crimes against persons with disabilities, several different methods have been used to calculate age-adjusted rates. More specifically, changes in the standard population were made. Over the years, the population without disabilities and the 2000 U.S. standard population generated by the U.S. Census Bureau have both been used as the standard population in calculating age-adjusted rates for persons with and without disabilities. Each time a change was made to the standard population, rates for all years were recalculated using the new standard population. This resulted in previous years having different rates from earlier reports.

In this report, BJS changed the calculation of victimization rates by disability status. For each year, unadjusted rates were calculated for persons with disabilities. For persons without disabilities, rates were age adjusted to the population of with disabilities for that year. For example, the 2012–2013 rate of violent victimization against persons with disabilities was unadjusted. The 2012–2013 rate of violent victimization for persons without disabilities was age adjusted using the 2012–2013 population with disabilities as the standard population.

Nonresponse and weighting adjustments

In 2013, about 90,630 households and 160,040 persons age 12 or older were interviewed for the NCVS. Each household was interviewed twice during the year. The response rate was 84% for households and 88% for eligible persons. Victimizations that occurred outside of the United States were excluded from this report. In 2013, less than 1% of the unweighted victimizations occurred outside of the United States and were excluded from the analyses.

Estimates in this report use data from the 2008 to 2013 NCVS data files weighted to produce annual estimates for persons age 12 or older living in U.S. households. Because the NCVS relies on a sample rather than a census of the entire U.S. population, weights are designed to inflate sample point estimates to known population totals and to compensate for survey nonresponse and other aspects of the sample design.

The NCVS data files include both household and person weights. The household weight is commonly used to calculate estimates of property crimes, such as motor vehicle theft or burglary, which are identified with the household. Person weights provide an estimate of the population represented by each person in the sample. Person weights are most frequently used to compute estimates of crime victimizations of persons in the total population. After proper adjustment, both household and person weights are also used to form the denominator in calculations of crime rates.

The victimization weights used in this analysis account for the number of persons present during an incident and for repeat victims of when a series of incidents occurs. The weight counts a series of incidents as the actual number of incidents reported by the victim, up to a maximum of 10 incidents. Series victimizations are victimizations that are similar in type but occur with such frequency that a victim is unable to recall each individual event or to describe each event in detail. Survey procedures allow NCVS interviewers to identify and classify these similar victimizations as series victimizations and collect detailed information on only the most recent incident in the series. In 2013, series incidents accounted for about 1% of all victimizations and 4% of all violent victimizations. The approach to weighting series incidents as the number of incidents up to a maximum of 10 produces more reliable estimates of crime levels, while the cap at 10 minimizes the effect of extreme outliers on the rates. Additional information on the series enumeration is detailed in the report *Methods for Counting High Frequency Repeat Victimizations in the National Crime Victimization Survey* (NCJ 237308, BJS web, April 2012).

Standard error computations for counts, percentages, and unadjusted rates

When national estimates are derived from a sample, as is the case with the NCVS, caution must be taken when comparing one estimate to another or when comparing estimates over time. Although one estimate may be larger than another, estimates based on a sample have some degree of sampling error. The sampling error of an estimate depends on several factors, including the amount of variation in the responses, the size of the sample, and the size of the subgroup for which the estimate is computed. When the sampling error around the estimates is taken into consideration, the estimates that appear different may not be statistically different.

One measure of the sampling error associated with an estimate is the standard error. The standard error can vary from one estimate to the next. In general, for a given metric, an estimate with a smaller standard error provides a more reliable approximation of the true value than an estimate with a larger standard error. Estimates with relatively large standard errors are associated with less precision and reliability and should be interpreted with caution.

To generate standard errors around numbers and estimates from the NCVS, the Census Bureau produces generalized variance function (GVF) parameters for BJS. The GVFs take into account aspects of the NCVS complex sample design and represent the curve fitted to a selection of individual standard errors based on the Jackknife Repeated Replication technique. The GVF parameters were used to generate standard errors for each point estimate (such as counts, percentages, and rates) in the report. For estimates, standard errors were based on the ratio of the sums of victimizations and respondents across years.

BJS conducted tests to determine whether differences in estimated numbers, percentages, and unadjusted rates in this report were statistically significant once sampling error was taken into account. Using statistical programs developed specifically for the NCVS, all comparisons in the text were tested for significance. The primary test procedure was the Student's t-statistic, which tests the difference between two sample estimates. Differences described as higher, lower, or different passed a test at the 0.05 level of statistical significance (95% confidence level). Differences described as somewhat, slightly, or marginally different, or with some indication of difference, passed a test at the 0.10 level of statistical significance (90% confidence level). Caution is required when comparing estimates not explicitly discussed in this report.

Data users can use the estimates and the standard errors of the estimates provided in this report to generate a confidence interval around the estimate as a measure of the margin of error. The following example illustrates how standard errors can be used to generate confidence intervals:

According to the NCVS, during 2012 and 2013, 50.3% of simple assault against persons with disabilities involved victims with multiple disability types (see table 8). Using the GVFs, BJS determined that the estimate has a standard error of 3.9% (see appendix table 10). A confidence interval around the estimate was generated by multiplying the standard errors by ±1.96 (the t-score of a normal, two-tailed distribution that excludes 2.5% at either end of the distribution). Therefore, the confidence interval around the 50.3% estimate from 2012 and 2013 is 50.3% + 3.9% x ± 1.96 (or 42.6% to 58.1%). In other words, if different samples using the same procedures were taken from the U.S. population during 2012 and 2013, 95% of the time the percentage of violent crimes against persons with disabilities in which the victim had multiple disability types would fall between 42.6% and 58.1%.

In this report, a coefficient of variation (CV), representing the ratio of the standard error to the estimate, was also calculated for all estimates. CVs provide a measure of reliability and a means for comparing the precision of estimates across measures with differing levels or metrics. In cases where the CV was greater than 50%, or the unweighted sample had 10 or fewer cases, the estimate was noted with a "!" symbol (Interpret data with caution. Estimate based on 10 or fewer sample cases, or coefficient of variation is greater than 50%.)

Standard error computations and statistical significance for age-adjusted rates

Due to the complexity in generating age-adjusted rates of violent crime, other methods were used to compute standard errors and determine statistical significance.[2] The standard error for age-adjusted rates was calculated as—

$$S_d = \sqrt{\Sigma\, (w_a{}^2 * v_a)}$$

where

S_d = standard error for an age-adjusted weight that was computed using direct standardization

w_a = weight calculated from the population with disabilities for age-group a

v_a = variance calculated age-group-specific rate using information from the generalized variance function (GVF) parameters that the Census Bureau produced for the NCVS.

To calculate statistical significance among two age-adjusted rates, the standard errors for the two rates were calculated using the formula above. A Student's t-statistic also was calculated, which tests the difference between two sample

estimates. Differences described as higher, lower, or different passed a test at the 0.05 level of statistical significance (95% confidence level). Differences described as somewhat, slightly, or marginally different, or with some indication of difference, passed a test at the 0.10 level of statistical significance (90% confidence level).

Property crime

Measuring property crime against households with persons with disabilities is difficult using the National Crime Victimization Survey (NCVS) due to the nature of capturing property crimes and the placement of the disability questions on the NCVS incident form (NCVS-2). In the NCVS, only the household respondent is asked about property crimes for the entire household. If the household has experienced a property crime, the household respondent is asked about various characteristics defined in the NCVS-2, including their disability status. The household respondent is not asked about the disability status of anyone else in the household. If the household respondent does not report having a disability, the NCVS cannot be used to determine if anyone else in the household has a disability. As a result, property crime by disability status in not included in this report.

---

[2]For more information on computing standard errors for age-adjusted rates, see Anderson, R.N., & Rosenberg, H.M. (1998). Age standardization of death rates: Implementation of the year 2000 standard. *National Vital Statistics Reports, 47* (3). Available at http://www.cdc.gov/nchs/data/nvsr/nvsr47/nvs47_03.pdf.

Crime Victims with Disabilities Awareness Act (Public Law 105-301), 1998

The Crime Victims with Disabilities Awareness Act mandates that the National Crime Victimization Survey (NCVS) include statistics on crimes against people with disabilities and the characteristics of these victims. The act was designed "to increase public awareness of the plight of victims of crime with developmental disabilities, to collect data to measure the magnitude of the problem, and to develop strategies to address the safety and justice needs of victims of crime with developmental disabilities." Section 5 of the act directed the Department of Justice to include statistics relating to "the nature of crimes against people with developmental disabilities; and the specific characteristics of the victims of those crimes" in the NCVS. This report is a part of the Bureau of Justice Statistics' (BJS) series on crime against people with disabilities. More information can be found on the BJS website.

APPENDIX TABLE 1
Estimates for figure 1: Annual number of violent victimizations, by victim's disability status, 2008–2013

Type of crime	Persons with disabilities						Persons without disabilities					
	2008	2009	2010	2011	2012	2013	2008	2009	2010	2011	2012	2013
Total	999,700	998,400	742,800	1,104,700	1,346,900	1,299,500	5,393,800	4,670,800	4,193,200	4,705,000	5,495,700	4,823,800
Serious violent crime	316,500	304,700	371,200	431,900	508,300	518,000	1,682,200	1,665,200	1,323,600	1,420,100	1,576,300	1,422,000
Rape/sexual assault	56,200	32,400	34,800	82,800	80,100	65,500	293,400	273,200	233,800	161,400	266,700	234,600
Robbery	145,000	125,500	156,800	130,700	233,000	159,100	534,800	509,600	411,700	426,500	508,800	486,500
Aggravated assault	115,200	146,800	179,700	218,400	195,200	293,400	854,000	882,500	678,100	832,200	800,900	700,800
Simple assault	683,300	693,700	371,600	672,800	838,600	781,500	3,711,500	3,005,600	2,869,600	3,284,800	3,919,300	3,401,800

Source: Bureau of Justice Statistics, National Crime Victimization Survey, 2008–2013.

APPENDIX TABLE 2
Standard errors for figure 1: Annual number of violent victimizations, by victim's disability status, 2008–2013

Type of crime	Persons with disabilities						Persons without disabilities					
	2008	2009	2010	2011	2012	2013	2008	2009	2010	2011	2012	2013
Total	126,923	138,611	109,163	128,665	132,644	165,557	391,578	403,394	370,747	353,077	339,005	418,042
Serious violent crime	60,203	61,651	66,974	67,166	70,218	86,299	179,317	197,496	164,317	153,286	147,215	176,483
Rape/sexual assault	20,937	14,533	13,370	22,209	22,407	20,648	57,388	57,289	48,501	34,481	46,630	49,503
Robbery	36,978	34,243	36,782	29,974	42,857	37,810	84,291	87,351	72,025	66,594	70,257	82,561
Aggravated assault	32,130	37,944	40,413	42,230	38,408	57,862	114,412	127,299	102,352	105,659	94,254	106,858
Simple assault	98,853	107,876	67,019	91,179	97,128	115,427	304,751	297,446	284,002	275,134	270,408	327,156

Source: Bureau of Justice Statistics, National Crime Victimization Survey, 2008–2013.

APPENDIX TABLE 3
Standard errors for table 1: Rates of violent victimizations, by victim's disability status and age, 2009–2013

Age of victim	Rate per 1,000 persons with disabilities					Rate per 1,000 persons without disabilities				
	2009	2010	2011	2012	2013	2009	2010	2011	2012	2013
Total	3.0	2.7	2.5	2.6	3.1	1.5	1.4	1.3	1.2	1.4
12–15	23.6	16.6	15.8	19.4	25.6	5.4	4.2	3.5	3.9	5.2
16–19	19.2	20.0	20.1	17.3	16.8	4.5	3.8	3.9	3.7	4.0
20–24	21.3	15.8	17.3	15.7	16.6	4.4	3.8	3.4	3.2	3.4
25–34	10.8	8.6	9.3	11.0	11.0	3.1	2.9	2.6	2.2	2.8
35–49	8.2	7.2	5.9	6.9	7.9	2.0	1.8	1.7	1.7	2.0
50–64	4.3	3.9	3.1	3.4	5.1	1.5	1.4	1.3	1.1	1.4
65 or older	1.0	0.8	1.0	1.1	1.0	1.0	0.9	0.7	0.8	0.9

Sources: Bureau of Justice Statistics, National Crime Victimization Survey, 2008–2013; and U.S. Census Bureau, American Community Survey, 2008–2013.

APPENDIX TABLE 4
Standard errors for table 2: Rates of violent victimization against persons with and without disabilities, by type of crime, 2009–2013

Type of crime	Unadjusted rate per 1,000 persons with disabilities					Age-adjusted rate per 1,000 persons without disabilities				
	2009	2010	2011	2012	2013	2009	2010	2011	2012	2013
Total	3.0	2.7	2.5	2.6	3.1	0.7	0.7	0.6	0.6	0.7
Serious violent crime	1.3	1.4	1.4	1.4	1.6	0.3	0.3	0.3	0.3	0.3
Rape/sexual assault	0.4	0.3	0.4	0.4	0.4	0.1	0.1	0.1	0.1	0.1
Robbery	0.8	0.8	0.7	0.8	0.9	0.1	0.2	0.1	0.1	0.1
Aggravated assault	0.8	0.8	0.9	0.8	0.9	0.2	0.2	0.2	0.2	0.2
Simple assault	2.3	1.8	1.7	1.8	2.2	0.6	0.5	0.4	0.5	0.5

Sources: Bureau of Justice Statistics, National Crime Victimization Survey, 2008–2013; and U.S. Census Bureau, American Community Survey, 2008–2013.

APPENDIX TABLE 5
Standard errors for table 3: Rates of violent victimization against persons with and without disabilities, by victim characteristics, 2009–2013

Victim characteristic	Unadjusted rate per 1,000 persons with disabilities					Age-adjusted rate per 1,000 persons without disabilities				
	2009	2010	2011	2012	2013	2009	2010	2011	2012	2013
Total	3.0	2.7	2.5	2.6	3.1	0.7	0.7	0.6	0.6	0.7
Sex										
Male	3.6	3.2	3.1	3.5	4.0	1.0	0.9	0.8	0.8	0.9
Female	3.9	3.4	3.1	3.0	3.8	0.9	0.8	0.6	0.7	0.8
Race										
White	3.2	2.8	2.6	2.8	3.5	0.8	0.7	0.6	0.6	0.7
Black	6.3	5.3	4.5	4.6	5.4	2.2	1.8	1.5	1.7	2.0
Other	7.3	4.6	5.4	5.8	4.5	1.0	0.8	0.6	0.8	1.0
Two or more races	18.1	19.5	18.1	15.9	17.4	4.8	3.2	4.1	3.6	3.2
Hispanic/Latino origin										
Hispanic/Latino	5.3	5.4	4.9	4.9	6.3	1.6	1.3	1.2	1.3	1.4
Non-Hispanic/Non-Latino	3.2	2.8	2.6	2.7	3.3	0.8	0.7	0.6	0.6	0.7

Sources: Bureau of Justice Statistics, National Crime Victimization Survey, 2008–2013; and U.S. Census Bureau, American Community Survey, 2008–2013.

APPENDIX TABLE 6
Standard errors for table 4: Rates of violent victimization against persons with disabilities, by disability type, 2009–2013

Disability type	2009	2010	2011	2012	2013
Hearing	3.3	2.2	2.8	2.8	2.9
Vision	5.3	4.6	3.9	3.8	4.8
Ambulatory	3.0	2.7	2.7	2.9	3.5
Cognitive	5.6	5.2	5.2	5.2	6.3
Self-care	4.0	3.5	4.2	3.8	4.2
Independent living	3.7	3.7	3.3	3.1	4.0

Sources: Bureau of Justice Statistics, National Crime Victimization Survey, 2008–2013; and U.S. Census Bureau, American Community Survey, 2008–2013.

APPENDIX TABLE 7
Standard errors for table 5: Rates of serious violent victimization against persons with disabilities, by disability type, 2009–2013

Disability type	2009	2010	2011	2012	2013
Hearing	1.8	1.2	1.6	1.9	1.8
Vision	2.4	2.8	2.3	1.9	2.6
Ambulatory	1.3	1.5	1.6	1.8	2.0
Cognitive	2.3	2.8	3.0	2.8	3.3
Self-care	1.5	2.0	2.4	2.2	2.1
Independent living	1.5	1.9	1.9	1.8	2.2

Sources: Bureau of Justice Statistics, National Crime Victimization Survey, 2008–2013; and U.S. Census Bureau, American Community Survey, 2008–2013.

APPENDIX TABLE 8
Standard errors for table 6: Rates of simple assault against persons with disabilities, by disability type, 2009–2013

Disability type	2009	2010	2011	2012	2013
Hearing	2.2	1.5	1.8	1.7	1.8
Vision	4.1	2.9	2.6	3.0	3.4
Ambulatory	2.2	1.8	1.7	1.9	2.3
Cognitive	4.5	3.5	3.3	3.8	4.6
Self-care	3.3	2.3	2.7	2.7	3.2
Independent living	3.0	2.6	2.1	2.2	2.7

Sources: Bureau of Justice Statistics, National Crime Victimization Survey, 2008–2013; and U.S. Census Bureau, American Community Survey, 2008–2013.

APPENDIX TABLE 9
Standard errors for table 7: Rates of violent victimization, by victim's sex and disability type, 2009–2013

Disability type	Rate per 1,000 males					Rate per 1,000 females				
	2009	2010	2011	2012	2013	2009	2010	2011	2012	2013
Hearing	2.8	2.7	3.6	3.6	3.2	6.0	3.1	3.3	3.5	4.4
Vision	7.8	6.4	4.9	5.0	5.4	6.2	5.2	5.0	4.9	6.6
Ambulatory	3.8	3.6	3.8	4.6	5.2	3.7	3.2	3.1	3.0	3.8
Cognitive	7.1	6.0	6.4	6.8	7.8	7.2	6.8	6.4	6.4	8.0
Self-care	5.7	4.3	6.3	6.0	5.4	4.8	4.5	4.5	4.1	5.4
Independent living	5.4	4.6	4.0	4.4	5.0	4.4	4.6	4.1	3.7	4.9

Sources: Bureau of Justice Statistics, National Crime Victimization Survey, 2008–2013; and U.S. Census Bureau, American Community Survey, 2008–2013.

APPENDIX TABLE 10
Standard errors for table 8: Percent of violence against persons with disabilities that involved victims with multiple disability types, by type of crime, 2009–2013

Type of crime	2009	2010	2011	2012	2013
Total	4.1%	4.1%	3.7%	3.0%	3.4%
Serious violent crime	5.6%	5.4%	4.5%	4.3%	4.5%
Rape/sexual assault	11.1	12.0	8.0	6.9	8.5
Robbery	7.1	7.4	6.5	6.2	6.1
Aggravated assault	8.3	6.7	5.9	5.8	5.4
Simple assault	4.5%	4.6%	4.2%	3.5%	3.9%

Source: Bureau of Justice Statistics, National Crime Victimization Survey, 2008–2013.

APPENDIX TABLE 11
Standard errors for table 9: Rates of violent victimization, by number of disability types and type of crime, 2009–2013

Type of crime	Persons with a single disability type					Persons with multiple disability types				
	2009	2010	2011	2012	2013	2009	2010	2011	2012	2013
Total	4.1	3.2	2.8	3.1	3.8	3.4	3.4	3.4	3.3	4.0
Serious violent crime	1.9	1.6	1.4	1.6	2.0	1.4	1.8	1.9	1.9	2.1
Rape/sexual assault	0.6	0.4	0.3	0.3	0.4	0.4	0.4	0.6	0.8	0.7
Robbery	1.2	1.0	0.7	1.0	1.2	0.7	1.0	1.0	1.0	0.9
Aggravated assault	1.0	0.9	1.0	1.0	1.0	1.0	1.1	1.2	1.1	1.3
Simple assault	3.1	2.2	1.9	2.3	2.7	2.7	2.3	2.2	2.3	2.8

Sources: Bureau of Justice Statistics, National Crime Victimization Survey, 2008–2013; and U.S. Census Bureau, American Community Survey, 2008–2013.

APPENDIX TABLE 12
Standard errors for table 10: Victim–offender relationship, by victim's disability status, 2009–2013

Victim–offender relationship	Persons with disabilities					Persons without disabilities				
	2009	2010	2011	2012	2013	2009	2010	2011	2012	2013
Intimate partner	3.2%	3.1%	2.2%	2.0%	2.2%	1.6%	1.6%	1.4%	1.1%	1.2%
Other relatives	2.2	1.6	2.0	1.7	1.6	0.9	0.9	0.9	0.7	0.8
Well known/casual acquaintances	3.8	3.9	3.4	2.8	3.3	2.1	2.1	1.9	1.7	2.0
Strangers	3.4	3.3	3.0	2.6	3.0	2.3	2.4	2.1	1.8	2.1
Don't know	2.0	1.8	1.7	1.3	1.0	1.3	1.0	1.0	0.9	1.0

Source: Bureau of Justice Statistics, National Crime Victimization Survey, 2008–2013.

APPENDIX TABLE 13
Standard errors for table 11: Time violent crime occurred, by victim's disability status, 2009–2013

Time of crime	Persons with disabilities					Persons without disabilities				
	2009	2010	2011	2012	2013	2009	2010	2011	2012	2013
Daytime (6 a.m.–6 p.m.)	4.2%	4.1%	3.6%	3.0%	3.4%	2.5%	2.5%	2.3%	1.9%	2.2%
Nighttime (6 p.m.–6 a.m.)	4.0	3.9	3.4	2.8	3.1	2.4	2.4	2.2	1.8	2.2
Don't know	1.9	1.2	0.9	1.2	1.4	0.7	0.7	0.6	0.5	0.5

Source: Bureau of Justice Statistics, National Crime Victimization Survey, 2008–2013.

APPENDIX TABLE 14
Standard errors for table 12: Percent of violent crime reported to police, by victim's disability status, 2009–2013

Victim's disability status	2009	2010	2011	2012	2013
Persons with disabilities	4.2%	4.0%	3.6%	3.0%	3.4%
Single disability type	5.1	5.1	4.8	3.9	4.3
Multiple disability types	5.7	5.1	4.2	3.7	4.3
Persons without disabilities	2.4%	2.5%	2.3%	1.9%	2.2%

Source: Bureau of Justice Statistics, National Crime Victimization Survey, 2008–2013.

APPENDIX TABLE 15
Standard errors for table 13: Person who notified police of violent crime, by victim's disability status, 2009–2013

Person who contacted police	Persons with disabilities					Persons without disabilities				
	2009	2010	2011	2012	2013	2009	2010	2011	2012	2013
Respondent	4.8%	4.4%	4.3%	3.8%	4.4%	3.2%	3.1%	2.8%	2.4%	2.9%
Other household member	2.3	1.4	1.3	1.2	1.7	1.7	1.5	1.5	1.4	1.4
Someone official	2.5	1.5	1.1	1.1	1.9	1.4	1.5	1.2	1.0	1.3
Someone else	2.9	2.5	3.0	3.0	3.4	1.8	1.5	1.3	1.4	1.7
Police were at the scene	1.2	1.6	1.1	1.3	1.4	1.2	1.1	0.8	1.0	1.2
Offender was a police officer	--	--	--	--	0.4	0.4	0.4	0.3	0.1	0.2
Some other way	0.7	1.1	1.3	1.1	1.1	0.5	0.4	0.6	0.6	0.6
Don't know	--	--	--	--	--	0.1	0.1	0.3	0.2	0.1

--Less than 0.05%.

Source: Bureau of Justice Statistics, National Crime Victimization Survey, 2008–2013.

APPENDIX TABLE 16
Standard errors for table 14: Reasons for not reporting violent crime to police, by victim's disability status, 2009–2013

Reason for not reporting crime to police	Persons with disabilities					Persons without disabilities				
	2009	2010	2011	2012	2013	2009	2010	2011	2012	2013
Dealt with another way	5.6%	4.7%	4.3%	3.7%	4.2%	2.8%	2.8%	2.7%	2.3%	2.6%
Not important enough to respondent	3.5	3.0	2.9	2.4	3.2	2.3	2.2	2.1	1.8	2.1
Insurance wouldn't cover	--	--	--	--	0.3	0.1	0.2	0.2	0.2	0.1
Police couldn't do anything	1.0	1.0	1.1	1.0	0.8	0.8	0.9	0.9	0.6	0.7
Police wouldn't help	4.8	4.8	3.5	2.8	3.1	2.2	2.3	1.9	1.8	2.0
Other reason	5.1	4.7	4.3	3.8	4.1	2.5	2.8	2.6	2.0	2.5

--Less than 0.05%.

Source: Bureau of Justice Statistics, National Crime Victimization Survey, 2008–2013.

APPENDIX TABLE 17
Standard errors for table 15: Percent of violent crime victims who received services from nonpolice victim services agencies, by victim's disability status, 2009–2013

Victim's disability status	2009	2010	2011	2012	2013
Persons with disabilities	2.7%	2.2%	2.0%	1.8%	1.9%
Persons without disabilities	1.0	1.0	0.9	0.8	1.0

Source: Bureau of Justice Statistics, National Crime Victimization Survey, 2008–2013.

APPENDIX TABLE 18

U.S. population, according to the U.S. Census Bureau's ACS PUMS data, by disability status and demographic characteristics, 2013

Demographic characteristic	Persons with disabilities		Persons without disabilities	
	Number	Percent of total	Number	Percent of total
Total	37,548,700	14.2%	226,131,900	85.8%
Sex				
Male	17,921,300	47.7%	110,203,500	48.7%
Female	19,627,300	52.3	115,928,300	51.3
Race[a]				
White	28,935,400	77.1%	168,962,300	74.7%
Black/African American	5,119,000	13.6	26,885,100	11.9
Other[b]	2,596,900	6.9	25,024,000	11.1
Two or more races	897,400	2.4	5,260,500	2.3
Hispanic/Latino origin[c]				
Hispanic/Latino	4,268,800	11.4%	36,998,900	16.4%
Non-Hispanic/Non-Latino	33,279,800	88.6	189,133,000	83.6
Age				
12–15	947,400	2.5%	15,718,500	7.0%
16–19	936,400	2.5	16,025,800	7.1
20–24	1,325,700	3.5	21,151,000	9.4
25–34	2,516,600	6.7	39,257,100	17.4
35–49	5,442,500	14.5	55,729,000	24.6
50–64	10,618,100	28.3	50,658,600	22.4
65 or older	15,762,000	42.0	27,592,000	12.2
Disability type[d]				
Hearing	10,803,700	28.8%	~	~
Vision	7,006,200	18.7	~	~
Ambulatory	20,470,500	54.5	~	~
Cognitive	13,491,500	35.9	~	~
Self-care	7,474,900	19.9	~	~
Independent living[e]	14,005,400	37.3	~	~

Note: Based on the noninstitutionalized U.S. residential population age 12 or older. Numbers rounded to the nearest hundred.

~Not applicable.

[a]Includes persons of Hispanic or Latino origin.

[b]Includes persons identified as American Indian or Alaska Native and Asian, Native Hawaiian, or other Pacific Islander.

[c]Includes persons of all races.

[d]Because of the allowance of multiple disability types, numbers and percentages sum to more than the total.

[e]Includes persons age 15 or older only.

Source: U.S. Census Bureau, American Community Survey, 2013.

APPENDIX TABLE 19
Rates of violent victimization against persons without disabilities, by type of crime, 2009–2013

Type of crime	2009	2010	2011	2012	2013
Total	23.3	20.2	20.0	22.7	22.9
Serious violent crime	7.7	6.8	6.2	6.7	6.6
Rape/sexual assault	1.3	1.2	0.9	1.0	1.1
Robbery	2.4	2.1	1.9	2.1	2.2
Aggravated assault	4.0	3.6	3.4	3.6	3.3
Simple assault	15.5	13.4	13.9	16.1	16.2

Note: Based on the noninstitutionalized U.S. residential population age 12 or older. Estimates were based on 2-year rolling averages. See appendix table 20 for standard errors.

Sources: Bureau of Justice Statistics, National Crime Victimization Survey, 2008–2013; and U.S. Census Bureau, American Community Survey, 2008–2013.

APPENDIX TABLE 20
Standard errors for appendix table 19: Rates of violent victimization against persons without disabilities, by type of crime, 2009–2013

Type of crime	2009	2010	2011	2012	2013
Total	1.5	1.4	1.3	1.2	1.4
Serious violent crime	0.7	0.6	0.5	0.5	0.6
Rape/sexual assault	0.2	0.2	0.1	0.1	0.2
Robbery	0.3	0.3	0.2	0.2	0.3
Aggravated assault	0.4	0.4	0.4	0.3	0.3
Simple assault	1.1	1.0	0.9	0.9	1.1

Sources: Bureau of Justice Statistics, National Crime Victimization Survey, 2008–2013; and U.S. Census Bureau, American Community Survey, 2008–2013.

APPENDIX TABLE 21
Rates of violent victimization against persons without disabilities, by victim characteristics, 2009–2013

Victim characteristic	2009	2010	2011	2012	2013
Total	23.3	20.2	20.0	22.7	22.9
Sex					
Male	24.8	21.2	22.5	25.9	24.8
Female	21.8	19.3	17.7	19.7	21.0
Race[a]					
White	24.2	20.4	20.5	23.4	23.4
Black	30.4	29.9	27.3	31.3	30.7
Other[b]	7.2	7.9	7.7	7.8	8.1
Two or more races	29.3	24.4	27.7	28.8	34.7
Hispanic/Latino origin[c]					
Hispanic/Latino	21.1	18.1	18.7	22.9	23.1
Non-Hispanic/Non-Latino	23.6	20.6	20.3	22.7	22.8

Note: Based on the noninstitutionalized U.S. residential population age 12 or older. Estimates are based on 2-year rolling averages. See appendix table 22 for standard errors.
[a]Includes persons of Hispanic or Latino origin.
[b]Includes persons identified as American Indian or Alaska Native and Asian, Native Hawaiian, or other Pacific Islander.
[c]Includes persons of all races.

Sources: Bureau of Justice Statistics, National Crime Victimization Survey, 2008–2013; and U.S. Census Bureau, American Community Survey, 2008–2013.

APPENDIX TABLE 22
Standard errors for appendix table 21: Rates of violent victimization against persons without disabilities, by victim characteristics, 2009–2013

Victim characteristic	2009	2010	2011	2012	2013
Total	1.5	1.4	1.3	1.2	1.4
Sex					
Male	2.0	1.7	1.7	1.5	1.8
Female	1.8	1.6	1.4	1.3	1.6
Race					
White	1.7	1.5	1.4	1.3	1.5
Black	3.5	3.3	2.8	2.7	3.1
Other	1.4	1.4	1.2	1.1	1.3
Two or more races	6.5	5.1	4.8	4.5	5.7
Hispanic/Latino origin					
Hispanic/Latino	2.5	2.2	2.0	2.0	2.4
Non-Hispanic/Non-Latino	1.6	1.5	1.3	1.2	1.5

Sources: Bureau of Justice Statistics, National Crime Victimization Survey, 2008–2013; and U.S. Census Bureau, American Community Survey, 2008–2013.

www.ingramcontent.com/pod-product-compliance
Lightning Source LLC
Chambersburg PA
CBHW080535190526
45169CB00008B/3181